THE ROO

THE DU

G000045013

THE ROOM and were first produce January 21, 1960, Theatre Club, and March 8, 1960, by the English Stage Company at the Royal Court Theatre.

Both plays immediately established the themes and the atmosphere which Pinter was to develop in his later work.

The photograph on the front cover showing Michael Brennan and Vivien Merchant in THE ROOM *is reproduced by courtesy of John Cowan. The portrait of Harold Pinter on the back is by Antony di Gesù.*

by the same author

BETRAYAL

THE BIRTHDAY PARTY

THE CARETAKER

THE COLLECTION *and* THE LOVER

THE HOMECOMING

THE HOTHOUSE

LANDSCAPE *and* SILENCE

NO MAN'S LAND

OLD TIMES

A SLIGHT ACHE *and* OTHER PLAYS

TEA PARTY *and* OTHER PLAYS

FIVE SCREENPLAYS

(The Servant, The Pumpkin Eater, The Quiller Memorandum, Accident, The Go-Between)

PLAYS: ONE

(The Birthday Party, The Room, The Dumb Waiter, A Slight Ache, A Night Out)

PLAYS: TWO

(The Caretaker, Night School, The Dwarfs, The Collection, The Lover)

PLAYS: THREE

(The Homecoming, Tea Party, The Basement, Landscape, Silence, six revue sketches)

PLAYS: FOUR

(Old Times, No Man's Land, Betrayal, Monologue, Family Voices)

THE PROUST SCREENPLAY

POEMS AND PROSE 1949–1977

THE ROOM

AND

THE DUMB WAITER

BY

Harold Pinter

LONDON
EYRE METHUEN LTD
11 NEW FETTER LANE EC4

TO VIVIEN

These plays are fully protected by copyright. All enquiries concerning performing rights or readings by amateurs should be directed to SAMUEL FRENCH LTD, 26 Southampton Street, Strand, London, W.C.2. Enquiries concerning professional performing rights or any other use of this material should be directed to the author's sole agents: ACTAC (Theatrical & Cinematic) LTD, 16 Cadogan Lane, London, S.W.1.

First published 1960
Copyright © 1959 and 1960
by Harold Pinter
Paperback edition first published 1966
Reprinted 1968, 1970, 1972, 1973 (twice), 1976 (twice), 1978, 1979 and 1981
Set, printed and bound in Great Britain by
Fakenham Press Ltd,
Fakenham, Norfolk
ISBN 0 413 30340 3

This paperback edition is sold subject to the condition that it shall not, by way of trade or otherwise, be lent, re-sold, hired out, or otherwise circulated without the publisher's prior consent in any form of binding or cover other than that in which it is published and without a similar condition including this condition being imposed on the subsequent purchaser.

Contents

THE ROOM was first presented at the Hampstead Theatre Club on 21st January, 1960, with the following cast:

BERT HUDD, *a man of fifty*	Howard Lang
ROSE, *a woman of sixty*	Vivien Merchant
MR KIDD, *an old man*	Henry Woolf
MR SANDS } *a young couple*	John Rees
MRS SANDS } *a young couple*	Auriol Smith
RILEY	Thomas Baptiste

Directed by Harold Pinter

THE ROOM was subsequently presented at the Royal Court Theatre on 8th March, 1960, with four changes in the cast:

BERT HUDD	Michael Brennan
MR KIDD	John Cater
MR SANDS	Michael Caine
MRS SANDS	Anne Bishop

Directed by Anthony Page

Scene: A room in a large house. A door down right. A gas-fire down left. A gas-stove and sink, up left. A window up centre. A table and chairs, centre. A rocking-chair, left centre. The foot of a double-bed protrudes from alcove, up right.

BERT *is at the table, wearing a cap, a magazine propped in front of him.* ROSE *is at the stove.*

ROSE. Here you are. This'll keep the cold out.

She places bacon and eggs on a plate, turns off the gas and takes the plate to the table.

It's very cold out, I can tell you. It's murder.

She returns to the stove and pours water from the kettle into the teapot, turns off the gas and brings the teapot to the table, pours salt and sauce on the plate and cuts two slices of bread. BERT *begins to eat.*

That's right. You eat that. You'll need it. You can feel it in here. Still, the room keeps warm. It's better than the basement, anyway.

She butters the bread.

I don't know how they live down there. It's asking for trouble. Go on. Eat it up. It'll do you good.

She goes to the sink, wipes a cup and saucer and brings them to the table.

If you want to go out you might as well have something inside you. Because you'll feel it when you get out.

She pours milk into the cup.

Just now I looked out of the window. It was enough for me. There wasn't a soul about. Can you hear the wind?

She sits in the rocking-chair.

I've never seen who it is. Who is it? Who lives down there? I'll have to ask. I mean, you might as well know, Bert. But whoever it is, it can't be too cosy.

Pause.

I think it's changed hands since I was last there. I didn't see who moved in then. I mean the first time it was taken.

Pause.

Anyway, I think they've gone now.

Pause.

But I think someone else has gone in now. I wouldn't like to live in that basement. Did you ever see the walls? They were running. This is all right for me. Go on, Bert. Have a bit more bread.

She goes to the table and cuts a slice of bread.

I'll have some cocoa on when you come back.

She goes to the window and settles the curtain.

No, this room's all right for me. I mean, you know where you are. When it's cold, for instance.

She goes to the table.

What about the rasher? Was it all right? It was a good one, I know, but not as good as the last lot I got in. It's the weather.

She goes to the rocking-chair, and sits.

Anyway, I haven't been out. I haven't been so well. I didn't feel up to it. Still, I'm much better today. I don't know about you though. I don't know whether you ought to go out. I mean, you shouldn't, straight after you've been laid up. Still. Don't worry, Bert. You go. You won't be long.

She rocks.

It's good you were up here, I can tell you. It's good you weren't down there, in the basement. That's no joke. Oh, I've left the tea. I've left the tea standing.

She goes to the table and pours tea into the cup.

No, it's not bad. Nice weak tea. Lovely weak tea. Here you are. Drink it down. I'll wait for mine. Anyway, I'll have it a bit stronger.

She takes a plate to the sink and leaves it.

Those walls would have finished you off. I don't know who lives down there now. Whoever it is, they're taking a big chance. Maybe they're foreigners.

She goes to the rocking-chair and sits.

I'd have pulled you through.

Pause.

There isn't room for two down there, anyway. I think there was one first, before he moved out. Maybe they've got two now.

She rocks.

If they ever ask you, Bert, I'm quite happy where I am. We're quiet, we're all right. You're happy up here. It's not far up either, when you come in from outside. And we're not bothered. And nobody bothers us.

Pause.

I don't know why you have to go out. Couldn't you run it down tomorrow? I could put the fire in later. You could sit by the fire. That's what you like, Bert, of an evening. It'll be dark in a minute as well, soon.

She rocks.

It gets dark now.

She rises and pours out tea at the table.

I made plenty. Go on.

She sits at table.

You looked out today? It's got ice on the roads. Oh, I know you can drive. I'm not saying you can't drive. I mentioned to Mr Kidd this morning that you'd be doing a run today. I told him you hadn't been too grand, but I said, still, he's a marvellous driver. I wouldn't mind what time, where, nothing, Bert. You know how to drive. I told him.

She wraps her cardigan about her.

But it's cold. It's really cold today, chilly. I'll have you some nice cocoa on for when you get back.

She rises, goes to the window, and looks out.

It's quiet. Be coming on for dark. There's no one about.

She stands, looking.

Wait a minute.

Pause.

I wonder who that is.

Pause.

No. I thought I saw someone.

Pause.

No.

She drops the curtain.

You know what though? It looks a bit better. It's not so windy. You'd better put on your thick jersey.

She goes to the rocking-chair, sits and rocks.

This is a good room. You've got a chance in a place like this. I look after you, don't I, Bert? Like when they offered us the basement here I said no straight off. I knew that'd be no good. The ceiling right on top of you. No, you've got a window here, you can move yourself, you can come home at night, if you have to go out, you can do your job, you can come home, you're all right. And I'm here. You stand a chance.

Pause.

I wonder who has got it now. I've never seen them, or heard of them. But I think someone's down there. Whoever's got it can keep it. That looked a good rasher, Bert. I'll have a cup of tea later. I like mine a bit stronger. You like yours weak.

A knock at the door. She stands.

Who is it?

Pause.

Hallo!

Knock repeated.

Come in then.

Knock repeated.

Who is it?

Pause. The door opens and MR KIDD *comes in.*

MR KIDD. I knocked.
ROSE. I heard you.
MR KIDD. Eh?
ROSE. We heard you.
MR KIDD. Hallo, Mr Hudd, how are you, all right? I've been looking at the pipes.
ROSE. Are they all right?

MR KIDD. Eh?

ROSE. Sit down, Mr Kidd.

MR KIDD. No, that's all right. I just popped in, like, to see how things were going. Well, it's cosy in here, isn't it?

ROSE. Oh, thank you, Mr Kidd.

MR KIDD. You going out today, Mr Hudd? I went out. I came straight in again. Only to the corner, of course.

ROSE. Not many people about today, Mr Kidd.

MR KIDD. So I thought to myself, I'd better have a look at those pipes. In the circumstances. I only went to the corner, for a few necessary items. It's likely to snow. Very likely, in my opinion.

ROSE. Why don't you sit down, Mr Kidd?

MR KIDD. No, no, that's all right.

ROSE. Well, it's a shame you have to go out in this weather, Mr Kidd. Don't you have a help?

MR KIDD. Eh?

ROSE. I thought you had a woman to help.

MR KIDD. I haven't got any woman.

ROSE. I thought you had one when we first came.

MR KIDD. No women here.

ROSE. Maybe I was thinking of somewhere else.

MR KIDD. Plenty of women round the corner. Not here though. Oh no. Eh, have I seen that before?

ROSE. What?

MR KIDD. That.

ROSE. I don't know. Have you?

MR KIDD. I seem to have some remembrance.

ROSE. It's just an old rocking-chair.

MR KIDD. Was it here when you came?

ROSE. No, I brought it myself.

MR KIDD. I could swear blind I've seen that before.

ROSE. Perhaps you have.

MR KIDD. What?

ROSE. I say, perhaps you have.

MR KIDD. Yes, maybe I have.

ROSE. Take a seat, Mr Kidd.

MR KIDD. I wouldn't take an oath on it though.

BERT *yawns and stretches, and continues looking at his magazine.*

No, I won't sit down, with Mr Hudd just having a bit of a rest after his tea. I've got to go and get mine going in a minute. You're going out then, Mr Hudd? I was just looking at your van. She's a very nice little van, that. I notice you wrap her up well for the cold. I don't blame you. Yes, I was hearing you go off, when was it, the other morning, yes. Very smooth. I can tell a good gear-change.

ROSE. I thought your bedroom was at the back, Mr Kidd.

MR KIDD. My bedroom?

ROSE. Wasn't it at the back? Not that I ever knew.

MR KIDD. I wasn't in my bedroom.

ROSE. Oh, well.

MR KIDD. I was up and about.

ROSE. I don't get up early in this weather. I can take my time. I take my time.

Pause.

MR KIDD. This was my bedroom.

ROSE. This? When?

MR KIDD. When I lived here.

ROSE. I didn't know that.

MR KIDD. I will sit down for a few ticks. (*He sits in the armchair.*)

ROSE. Well, I never knew that.

MR KIDD. Was this chair here when you came?

ROSE. Yes.

MR KIDD. I can't recollect this one.

Pause.

ROSE. When was that then?

MR KIDD. Eh?

ROSE. When was this your bedroom?

MR KIDD. A good while back.

Pause.

ROSE. I was telling Bert I was telling you how he could drive.

MR KIDD. Mr Hudd? Oh, Mr Hudd can drive all right. I've seen him bowl down the road all right. Oh yes.

ROSE. Well, Mr Kidd, I must say this is a very nice room. It's a very comfortable room.

MR KIDD. Best room in the house.

ROSE. It must get a bit damp downstairs.

MR KIDD. Not as bad as upstairs.

ROSE. What about downstairs?

MR KIDD. Eh?

ROSE. What about downstairs?

MR KIDD. What about it?

ROSE. Must get a bit damp.

MR KIDD. A bit. Not as bad as upstairs though.

ROSE. Why's that?

MR KIDD. The rain comes in.

Pause.

ROSE. Anyone live up there?

MR KIDD. Up there? There was. Gone now.

ROSE. How many floors you got in this house?

MR KIDD. Floors. (*He laughs.*) Ah, we had a good few of them in the old days.

ROSE. How many have you got now?

MR KIDD. Well, to tell you the truth, I don't count them now.

ROSE. Oh.

MR KIDD. No, not now.

ROSE. It must be a bit of a job.

MR KIDD. Oh, I used to count them, once. Never got tired of it. I used to keep a tack on everything in this house. I had a lot to keep my eye on, then. I was able for it too. That was when my sister was alive. But I lost track a bit, after she died. She's been dead some time now, my sister. It was a good house then. She was a capable woman. Yes. Fine size of a woman too. I think she took after my mum. Yes, I think she took after my old mum, from what I can recollect. I think my mum was a Jewess. Yes, I wouldn't be surprised to learn that she was a Jewess. She didn't have many babies.

ROSE. What about your sister, Mr Kidd?

MR KIDD. What about her?

ROSE. Did she have any babies?

MR KIDD. Yes, she had a resemblance to my old mum, I think. Taller, of course.

ROSE. When did she die then, your sister?

MR KIDD. Yes, that's right, it was after she died that I must have stopped counting. She used to keep things in very good trim. And I gave her a helping hand. She was very grateful, right until her last. She always used to tell me how much she appreciated all the – little things – that I used to do for her. Then she copped it. I was her senior. Yes, I was her senior. She had a lovely boudoir. A beautiful boudoir.

ROSE. What did she die of?

MR KIDD. Who?

ROSE. Your sister.

Pause.

MR KIDD. I've made ends meet.

Pause.

ROSE. You full at the moment, Mr Kidd?

MR KIDD. Packed out.

ROSE. All sorts, I suppose?

MR KIDD. Oh yes, I make ends meet.

ROSE. We do, too, don't we, Bert?

Pause.

Where's your bedroom now then, Mr Kidd?

MR KIDD. Me? I can take my pick. (*Rising.*) You'll be going out soon then, Mr Hudd? Well, be careful how you go. Those roads'll be no joke. Still, you know how to manipulate your van all right, don't you? Where you going? Far? Be long?

ROSE. He won't be long.

MR KIDD. No, of course not. Shouldn't take him long.

ROSE. No.

MR KIDD. Well then, I'll pop off. Have a good run, Mr Hudd. Mind how you go. It'll be dark soon too. But not for a good while yet. Arivederci.

He exits.

ROSE. I don't believe he had a sister, ever.

She takes the plate and cup to the sink. BERT *pushes his chair back and rises.*

All right. Wait a minute. Where's your jersey?

She brings the jersey from the bed.

Here you are. Take your coat off. Get into it.

She helps him into his jersey.

Right. Where's your muffler?

She brings a muffler from the bed.

Here you are. Wrap it round. That's it. Don't go too fast, Bert, will you? I'll have some cocoa on when you get back. You won't be long. Wait a minute. Where's your overcoat? You'd better put on your overcoat.

He fixes his muffler, goes to the door and exits. She stands, watching the door, then turns slowly to the table, picks up the magazine, and puts it down. She stands and listens, goes to the fire, bends, lights the fire and warms her hands. She stands and looks about the room. She looks at the window and listens, goes quickly to the window, stops and straightens the curtain. She comes to the centre of the room, and looks towards the door. She goes to the bed, puts on a shawl, goes to the sink, takes a bin from under the sink, goes to the door and opens it.

ROSE. Oh!

MR *and* MRS SANDS *are disclosed on the landing.*

MRS SANDS. So sorry. We didn't mean to be standing here, like. Didn't mean to give you a fright. We've just come up the stairs.

ROSE. That's all right.

MRS SANDS. This is Mr Sands. I'm Mrs Sands.

ROSE. How do you do?

MR SANDS *grunts acknowledgement.*

MRS SANDS. We were just going up the stairs. But you can't see a thing in this place. Can you, Toddy?

MR SANDS. Not a thing.

ROSE. What were you looking for?

MRS SANDS. The man who runs the house.

MR SANDS. The landlord. We're trying to get hold of the landlord.

MRS SANDS. What's his name, Toddy?

ROSE. His name's Mr Kidd.

MRS SANDS. Kidd, Was that the name, Toddy?

MR SANDS. Kidd? No, that's not it.

ROSE. Mr Kidd. That's his name.

MR SANDS. Well, that's not the bloke we're looking for.

ROSE. Well, you must be looking for someone else.

Pause.

MR SANDS. I suppose we must be.

ROSE. You look cold.

MRS SANDS. It's murder out. Have you been out?

ROSE. No.

MRS SANDS. We've not long come in.

ROSE. Well, come inside, if you like, and have a warm.

They come into the centre of the room.

(*Bringing the chair from the table to the fire*). Sit down here. You can get a good warm.

MRS SANDS. Thanks. (*She sits.*)

ROSE. Come over by the fire, Mr. Sands.

MR SANDS. No, it's all right. I'll just stretch my legs.

MRS SANDS. Why? You haven't been sitting down.

MR SANDS. What about it?

MRS SANDS. Well, why don't you sit down?

MR SANDS. Why should I?

MRS SANDS. You must be cold.

MR SANDS. I'm not.

MRS SANDS. You must be. Bring over a chair and sit down.

MR SANDS. I'm all right standing up, thanks.

MRS SANDS. You don't look one thing or the other standing up.

MR SANDS. I'm quite all right, Clarissa.

ROSE. Clarissa? What a pretty name.

MRS SANDS. Yes, it is nice, isn't it? My father and mother gave it to me.

Pause.

You know, this is a room you can sit down and feel cosy in.

MR SANDS (*looking at the room*). It's a fair size, all right.

MRS SANDS. Why don't you sit down, Mrs –

ROSE. Hudd. No thanks.

MR SANDS. What did you say?

ROSE. When?

MR SANDS. What did you say the name was?

ROSE. Hudd.

MR SANDS. That's it. You're the wife of the bloke you mentioned then?

MRS SANDS. No, she isn't. That was Mr Kidd.
MR SANDS. Was it? I thought it was Hudd.
MRS SANDS. No, it was Kidd. Wasn't it, Mrs Hudd?
ROSE. That's right. The landlord.
MRS SANDS. No, not the landlord. The other man.
ROSE. Well, that's his name. He's the landlord.
MR SANDS. Who?
ROSE. Mr Kidd.

Pause.

MR SANDS. Is he?
MRS SANDS. Maybe there are two landlords.

Pause.

MR SANDS. That'll be the day.
MRS SANDS. What did you say?
MR SANDS. I said that'll be the day.

Pause.

ROSE. What's it like out?
MRS SANDS. It's very dark out.
MR SANDS. No darker than in.
MRS SANDS. He's right there.
MR SANDS. It's darker in than out, for my money.
MRS SANDS. There's not much light in this place, is there, Mrs Hudd? Do you know, this is the first bit of light we've seen since we came in?
MR SANDS. The first crack.
ROSE. I never go out at night. We stay in.
MRS SANDS. Now I come to think of it, I saw a star.
MR SANDS. You saw what?
MRS SANDS. Well, I think I did.
MR SANDS. You think you saw what?
MRS SANDS. A star.
MR SANDS. Where?
MRS SANDS. In the sky.

MR SANDS. When?

MRS SANDS. As we were coming along.

MR SANDS. Go home.

MRS SANDS. What do you mean?

MR SANDS. You didn't see a star.

MRS SANDS. Why not?

MR SANDS. Because I'm telling you. I'm telling you you didn't see a star.

Pause.

ROSE. I hope it's not too dark out. I hope it's not too icy. My husband's in his van. He doesn't drive slow either. He never drives slow.

MR SANDS (*guffawing*). Well, he's taking a big chance tonight then.

ROSE. What?

MR SANDS. No – I mean, it'd be a bit dodgy driving tonight.

ROSE. He's a very good driver.

Pause.

How long have you been here?

MRS SANDS. I don't know. How long have we been here, Toddy?

MR SANDS. About half an hour.

MRS SANDS. Longer than that, much longer.

MRS SANDS. About thirty-five minutes.

ROSE. Well, I think you'll find Mr Kidd about somewhere. He's not long gone to make his tea.

MR SANDS. He lives here, does he?

ROSE. Of course he lives here.

MR SANDS. And you say he's the landlord, is he?

ROSE. Of course he is.

MR SANDS. Well, say I wanted to get hold of him, where would I find him?

ROSE. Well – I'm not sure.

MR SANDS. He lives here, does he?

ROSE. Yes, but I don't know –

MR SANDS. You don't know exactly where he hangs out?

ROSE. No, not exactly.

MR SANDS. But he does live here, doesn't he?

Pause.

MRS SANDS. This is a very big house, Toddy.

MR SANDS. Yes, I know it is. But Mrs Hudd seems to know Mr Kidd very well.

ROSE. No, I wouldn't say that. As a matter of fact, I don't know him at all. We're very quiet. We keep ourselves to ourselves. I never interfere. I mean, why should I? We've got our room. We don't bother anyone else. That's the way it should be.

MRS SANDS. It's a nice house, isn't it? Roomy.

ROSE. I don't know about the house. We're all right, but I wouldn't mind betting there's a lot wrong with this house. (*She sits in the rocking-chair.*) I think there's a lot of damp.

MRS SANDS. Yes, I felt a bit of damp when we were in the basement just now.

ROSE. You were in the basement?

MRS SANDS. Yes, we went down there when we came in.

ROSE. Why?

MRS SANDS. We were looking for the landlord.

ROSE. What was it like down there?

MR SANDS. Couldn't see a thing.

ROSE. Why not?

MR SANDS. There wasn't any light.

ROSE. But what was – you said it was damp?

MRS SANDS. I felt a bit, didn't you, Tod?

MR SANDS. Why? Haven't you ever been down there, Mrs Hudd?

ROSE. Oh yes, once, a long time ago.

MR SANDS. Well, you know what it's like then, don't you?

ROSE It was a long time ago

MR SANDS. You haven't been here all that long, have you?

ROSE. I was just wondering whether anyone was living down there now.

MRS SANDS. Yes. A man.

ROSE. A man?

MRS SANDS. Yes.

ROSE. One man?

MR SANDS. Yes, there was a bloke down there, all right.

He perches on the table.

MRS SANDS. You're sitting down!

MR SANDS (*jumping up*). Who is?

MRS SANDS. You were.

MR SANDS. Don't be silly. I perched.

MRS SANDS. I saw you sit down.

MR SANDS. You did not see me sit down because I did not sit bloody well down. I perched!

MRS SANDS. Do you think I can't perceive when someone's sitting down?

MR SANDS. Perceive! That's all you do. Perceive.

MRS SANDS. You could do with a bit more of that instead of all that tripe you get up to.

MR SANDS. You don't mind some of that tripe!

MRS SANDS. You take after your uncle, that's who you take after!

MR SANDS. And who do you take after?

MRS SANDS (*rising*). I didn't bring you into the world.

MR SANDS. You didn't what?

MRS SANDS. I said, I didn't bring you into the world.

MR SANDS. Well, who did then? That's what I want to know. Who did? Who did bring me into the world?

She sits, muttering. He stands, muttering.

ROSE. You say you saw a man downstairs, in the basement?

MRS SANDS. Yes, Mrs Hudd, you see, the thing is, Mrs

Hudd, we'd heard they'd got a room to let here, so we thought we'd come along and have a look. Because we're looking for a place, you see, somewhere quiet, and we knew this district was quiet, and we passed the house a few months ago and we thought it looked very nice, but we thought we'd call of an evening, to catch the landlord, so we came along this evening. Well, when we got here we walked in the front door and it was very dark in the hall and there wasn't anyone about. So we went down to the basement. Well, we got down there only due to Toddy having such good eyesight really. Between you and me, I didn't like the look of it much, I mean the feel, we couldn't make much out, it smelt damp to me. Anyway, we went through a kind of partition, then there was another partition, and we couldn't see where we were going, well, it seemed to me it got darker the more we went, the further we went in, I thought we must have come to the wrong house. So I stopped. And Toddy stopped. And then this voice said, this voice came – it said – well, it gave me a bit of a fright, I don't know about Tod, but someone asked if he could do anything for us. So Tod said we were looking for the landlord and this man said the landlord would be upstairs. Then Tod asked was there a room vacant. And this man, this voice really, I think he was behind the partition, said yes there was a room vacant. He was very polite, I thought, but we never saw him, I don't know why they never put a light on. Anyway, we got out then and we came up and we went to the top of the house. I don't know whether it was the top. There was a door locked on the stairs, so there might have been another floor, but we didn't see anyone, and it was dark, and we were just coming down again when you opened your door.

ROSE. You said you were going up.

MRS SANDS. What?

ROSE. You said you were going up before.

MRS SANDS. No, we were coming down.

ROSE. You didn't say that before.

MRS SANDS. We'd been up.

MR SANDS. We'd been up. We were coming down.

Pause.

ROSE. This man, what was he like, was he old?

MRS SANDS. We didn't see him.

ROSE. Was he old?

Pause.

MR SANDS. Well, we'd better try to get hold of this landlord, if he's about.

ROSE. You won't find any rooms vacant in this house.

MR SANDS. Why not?

ROSE. Mr Kidd told me. He told me.

MR SANDS. Mr Kidd?

ROSE. He told me he was full up.

MR SANDS. The man in the basement said there was one. One room. Number seven he said.

Pause.

ROSE. That's this room.

MR SANDS. We'd better go and get hold of the landlord.

MRS SANDS (*rising*). Well, thank you for the warm-up, Mrs Hudd. I feel better now.

ROSE. This room is occupied.

MR SANDS. Come on.

MRS SANDS. Goodnight, Mrs Hudd. I hope your husband won't be too long. Must be lonely for you, being all alone here.

MR SANDS. Come on.

They go out. ROSE *watches the door close, starts towards it, and stops. She takes the chair back to the table, picks up the magazine, looks at it, and puts it down. She goes to the rocking-chair, sits, rocks, stops, and sits still. There is a sharp knock at the door, which opens. Enter* MR KIDD.

MR KIDD. I came straight in.

ROSE (*rising*). Mr Kidd! I was just going to find you. I've got to speak to you.

MR KIDD. Look here, Mrs Hudd, I've got to speak to you. I came up specially.

ROSE. There were two people in here just now. They said this room was going vacant. What were they talking about?

MR KIDD. As soon as I heard the van go I got ready to come and see you. I'm knocked out.

ROSE. What was it all about? Did you see those people? How can this room be going? It's occupied. Did they get hold of you, Mr Kidd?

MR KIDD. Get hold of me? Who?

ROSE. I told you. Two people. They were looking for the landlord.

MR KIDD. I'm just telling you. I've been getting ready to come and see you, as soon as I heard the van go.

ROSE. Well then, who were they?

MR KIDD. That's why I came up before. But he hadn't gone yet. I've been waiting for him to go the whole week-end.

ROSE. Mr Kidd, what did they mean about this room?

MR KIDD. What room?

ROSE. Is this room vacant?

MR KIDD. Vacant?

ROSE. They were looking for the landlord.

MR KIDD. Who were?

ROSE. Listen, Mr Kidd, you are the landlord, aren't you? There isn't any other landlord?

MR KIDD. What? What's that got to do with it? I don't know what you're talking about. I've got to tell you, that's all. I've got to tell you. I've had a terrible week-end. You'll have to see him. I can't take it any more. You've got to see him.

Pause.

ROSE. Who?

MR KIDD. The man. He's been waiting to see you. He wants to see you. I can't get rid of him. I'm not a young man, Mrs Hudd, that's apparent. It's apparent. You've got to see him.

ROSE. See who?

MR KIDD. The man. He's downstairs now. He's been there the whole week-end. He said that when Mr Hudd went out I was to tell him. That's why I came up before. But he hadn't gone yet. So I told him. I said he hasn't gone yet. I said, well when he goes, I said, you can go up, go up, have done with it. No, he says, you must ask her if she'll see me. So I came up again, to ask you if you'll see him.

ROSE. Who is he?

MR KIDD. How do I know who he is? All I know is he won't say a word, he won't indulge in any conversation, just – has he gone? that and nothing else. He wouldn't even play a game of chess. All right, I said, the other night, while we're waiting I'll play you a game of chess. You play chess, don't you? I tell you, Mrs Hudd, I don't know if he even heard what I was saying. He just lies there. It's not good for me. He just lies there, that's all, waiting.

ROSE. He lies there, in the basement?

MR KIDD. Shall I tell him it's all right, Mrs Hudd?

ROSE. But it's damp down there.

MR KIDD. Shall I tell him it's all right?

ROSE. That what's all right?

MR KIDD. That you'll see him.

ROSE. See him? I beg your pardon, Mr Kidd. I don't know him. Why should I see him?

MR KIDD. You won't see him?

ROSE. Do you expect me to see someone I don't know? With my husband not here too?

MR KIDD. But he knows you, Mrs Hudd, he knows you.

ROSE. How could he, Mr Kidd, when I don't know him?

MR KIDD. You must know him.

ROSE. But I don't know anybody. We're quiet here. We've just moved into this district.

MR KIDD. But he doesn't come from this district. Perhaps you knew him in another district.

ROSE. Mr Kidd, do you think I go around knowing men in one district after another? What do you think I am?

MR KIDD. I don't know what I think.

He sits.

I think I'm going off my squiff.

ROSE. You need rest. An old man like you. What you need is rest.

MR KIDD. He hasn't given me any rest. Just lying there. In the black dark. Hour after hour. Why don't you leave me be, both of you? Mrs Hudd, have a bit of pity. Please see him. Why don't you see him?

ROSE. I don't know him.

MR KIDD. You can never tell. You might know him.

ROSE. I don't know him.

MR KIDD (*rising*). I don't know what'll happen if you don't see him.

ROSE. I've told you I don't know this man!

MR KIDD. I know what he'll do. I know what he'll do. If you don't see him now, there'll be nothing else for it, he'll come up on his own bat, when your husband's here, that's what he'll do. He'll come up when Mr Hudd's here, when your husband's here.

ROSE. He'd never do that.

MR KIDD. He would do that. That's exactly what he'll do. You don't think he's going to go away without seeing you, after he's come all this way, do you? You don't think that, do you?

ROSE. All this way?

MR KIDD. You don't think he's going to do that, do you?

Pause.

ROSE. He wouldn't do that.

MR KIDD. Oh yes. I know it.

Pause.

ROSE. What's the time?

MR KIDD. I don't know.

Pause.

ROSE. Fetch him. Quick. Quick!

MR KIDD *goes out. She sits in the rocking-chair.*
After a few moments the door opens. Enter a blind Negro. He closes the door behind him, walks further, and feels with a stick till he reaches the armchair. He stops.

RILEY. Mrs Hudd?

ROSE. You just touched a chair. Why don't you sit in it?

He sits.

RILEY. Thank you.

ROSE. Don't thank me for anything. I don't want you up here. I don't know who you are. And the sooner you get out the better.

Pause.

(*Rising.*) Well, come on. Enough's enough. You can take a liberty too far, you know. What do you want? You force your way up here. You disturb my evening. You come in and sit down here. What do you want?

He looks about the room.

What are you looking at? You're blind, aren't you? So what are you looking at? What do you think you've got here, a little girl? I can keep up with you. I'm one ahead of people like you. Tell me what you want and get out.

RILEY. My name is Riley.

ROSE. I don't care if it's – What? That's not your name. That's not your name. You've got a grown-up woman in this room, do you hear? Or are you deaf too? You're not deaf too, are you? You're all deaf and dumb and blind, the lot of you. A bunch of cripples.

Pause.

RILEY. This is a large room.

ROSE. Never mind about the room. What do you know about this room? You know nothing about it. And you won't be staying in it long either. My luck. I get these creeps come in, smelling up my room. What do you want?

RILEY. I want to see you.

ROSE. Well you can't see me, can you? You're a blind man. An old, poor blind man. Aren't you? Can't see a dickeybird.

Pause.

They say I know you. That's an insult, for a start. Because I can tell you, I wouldn't know you to spit on, not from a mile off.

Pause.

Oh, these customers. They come in here and stink the place out. After a handout. I know all about it. And as for you saying you know me, what liberty is that? Telling my landlord too. Upsetting my landlord. What do you think you're up to? We're settled down here, cosy, quiet, and our landlord thinks the world of us, we're his favourite tenants, and you come in and drive him up the wall, and drag my name into it! What did you mean by dragging my name into it, and my husband's name? How did you know what our name was?

Pause.

You've led him a dance, have you, this week-end? You've got him going, have you? A poor, weak old man, who lets a respectable house. Finished. Done for. You push your way in and shove him about. And you drag my name into it.

Pause.

Come on, then. You say you wanted to see me. Well, I'm here. Spit it out or out you go. What do you want?

RILEY. I have a message for you.

ROSE. You've got what? How could you have a message for me, Mister Riley, when I don't know you and nobody knows I'm here and I don't know anybody anyway. You think I'm an easy touch, don't you? Well, why don't you give it up as a bad job? Get off out of it. I've had enough of this. You're not only a nut, you're a blind nut and you can get out the way you came.

Pause.

What message? Who have you got a message from? Who?

RILEY. Your father wants you to come home.

Pause.

ROSE. Home?

RILEY. Yes.

ROSE. Home? Go now. Come on. It's late. It's late.

RILEY. To come home.

ROSE. Stop it. I can't take it. What do you want? What do you want?

RILEY. Come home, Sal.

Pause.

ROSE. What did you call me?

RILEY. Come home, Sal.

ROSE. Don't call me that.

RILEY. Come, now.

ROSE. Don't call me that.

RILEY. So now you're here.

ROSE. Not Sal.

RILEY. Now I touch you.

ROSE. Don't touch me.

RILEY. Sal.

ROSE. I can't.

RILEY. I want you to come home.

ROSE. No.

RILEY. With me.
ROSE. I can't.
RILEY. I waited to see you.
ROSE. Yes.
RILEY. Now I see you.
ROSE. Yes.
RILEY. Sal.
ROSE. Not that.
RILEY. So, now.

Pause.

So, now.
ROSE. I've been here.
RILEY. Yes.
ROSE. Long.
RILEY. Yes.
ROSE. The day is a hump. I never go out.
RILEY. No.
ROSE. I've been here.
RILEY. Come home now, Sal.

She touches his eyes, the back of his head and his temples with her hands. Enter BERT.

He stops at the door, then goes to the window and draws the curtains. It is dark. He comes to the centre of the room and regards the woman.

BERT. I got back all right.
ROSE (*going towards him*). Yes.
BERT. I got back all right.

Pause.

ROSE. Is it late?
BERT. I had a good bowl down there.

Pause.

I drove her down, hard. They got it dark out.
ROSE. Yes.

BERT. Then I drove her back, hard. They got it very icy out.
ROSE. Yes.
BERT. But I drove her.

Pause.

I sped her.

Pause.

I caned her along. She was good. Then I got back. I could see the road all right. There was no cars. One there was. He wouldn't move. I bumped him. I got my road. I had all my way. There again and back. They shoved out of it. I kept on the straight. There was no mixing it. Not with her. She was good. She went with me. She don't mix it with me. I use my hand. Like that. I get hold of her. I go where I go. She took me there. She brought me back.

Pause.

I got back all right.

He takes the chair from the table and sits to the left of the NEGRO'S *chair, close to it. He regards the* NEGRO *for some moments. Then with his foot he lifts the armchair up. The* NEGRO *falls on to the floor. He rises slowly.*

RILEY. Mr Hudd, your wife –
BERT. Lice!

He strikes the NEGRO, *knocking him down, and then kicks his head against the gas-stove several times. The* NEGRO *lies still.* BERT *walks away.*
Silence.
ROSE *stands clutching her eyes.*

ROSE. Can't see. I can't see. I can't see.

Blackout

Curtain

The Dumb Waiter

THE DUMB WAITER was first presented at the Hampstead Theatre Club on 21st January, 1960, with the following cast:

BEN Nicholas Selby
GUS George Tovey

THE DUMB WAITER was subsequently presented at the Royal Court Theatre on 8th March, 1960, with the same cast.
Directed by James Roose-Evans

Scene: A basement room. Two beds, flat against the back wall. A serving hatch, closed, between the beds. A door to the kitchen and lavatory, left. A door to a passage, right.

BEN *is lying on a bed, left, reading a paper.* GUS *is sitting on a bed, right, tying his shoelaces, with difficulty. Both are dressed in shirts, trousers and braces.*

Silence.

GUS *ties his laces, rises, yawns and begins to walk slowly to the door, left. He stops, looks down, and shakes his foot.*

BEN *lowers his paper and watches him.* GUS *kneels and unties his shoe-lace and slowly takes off the shoe. He looks inside it and brings out a flattened matchbox. He shakes it and examines it. Their eyes meet.* BEN *rattles his paper and reads.* GUS *puts the matchbox in his pocket and bends down to put on his shoe. He ties his lace, with difficulty.* BEN *lowers his paper and watches him.* GUS *walks to the door, left, stops, and shakes the other foot. He kneels, unties his shoe-lace, and slowly takes off the shoe. He looks inside it and brings out a flattened cigarette packet. He shakes it and examines it. Their eyes meet.* BEN *rattles his paper and reads.* GUS *puts the packet in his pocket, bends down, puts on his shoe and ties the lace.*

He wanders off, left.

BEN *slams the paper down on the bed and glares after him. He picks up the paper and lies on his back, reading.*

Silence.

A lavatory chain is pulled twice off, left, but the lavatory does not flush.

Silence.

GUS *re-enters, left, and halts at the door, scratching his head.*

BEN *slams down the paper.*

BEN. Kaw!

He picks up the paper.

What about this? Listen to this!

He refers to the paper.

A man of eighty-seven wanted to cross the road. But there was a lot of traffic, see? He couldn't see how he was going to squeeze through. So he crawled under a lorry.

GUS. He what?

BEN. He crawled under a lorry. A stationary lorry.

GUS. No?

BEN. The lorry started and ran over him.

GUS. Go on!

BEN. That's what it says here.

GUS. Get away.

BEN. It's enough to make you want to puke, isn't it?

GUS. Who advised him to do a thing like that?

BEN. A man of eighty-seven crawling under a lorry!

GUS. It's unbelievable.

BEN. It's down here in black and white.

GUS. Incredible.

Silence.

GUS *shakes his head and exits.* BEN *lies back and reads.* *The lavatory chain is pulled once off left, but the lavatory does not flush.*

BEN *whistles at an item in the paper.*

GUS *re-enters.*

I want to ask you something.

BEN. What are you doing out there?

GUS. Well, I was just –

BEN. What about the tea?

GUS. I'm just going to make it.

BEN. Well, go on, make it.

GUS. Yes, I will. (*He sits in a chair. Ruminatively.*) He's laid on some very nice crockery this time, I'll say that. It's sort of striped. There's a white stripe.

BEN *reads.*

It's very nice. I'll say that.

BEN *turns the page.*

You know, sort of round the cup. Round the rim. All the rest of it's black, you see. Then the saucer's black, except for right in the middle, where the cup goes, where it's white.

BEN *reads.*

Then the plates are the same, you see. Only they've got a black stripe – the plates – right across the middle. Yes, I'm quite taken with the crockery.

BEN (*still reading*). What do you want plates for? You're not going to eat.

GUS. I've brought a few biscuits.

BEN. Well, you'd better eat them quick.

GUS. I always bring a few biscuits. Or a pie. You know I can't drink tea without anything to eat.

BEN. Well, make the tea then, will you? Time's getting on.

GUS *brings out the flattened cigarette packet and examines it.*

GUS. You got any cigarettes? I think I've run out.

He throws the packet high up and leans forward to catch it.

I hope it won't be a long job, this one.

Aiming carefully, he flips the packet under his bed.

Oh, I wanted to ask you something.

BEN (*slamming his paper down*). Kaw!

GUS. What's that?

BEN. A child of eight killed a cat!

GUS. Get away.

BEN. It's a fact. What about that, eh? A child of eight killing a cat!

GUS. How did he do it?

BEN. It was a girl.

GUS. How did she do it?

BEN. She –

He picks up the paper and studies it.

It doesn't say.

GUS. Why not?

BEN. Wait a minute. It just says – Her brother, aged eleven, viewed the incident from the toolshed.

GUS. Go on!

BEN. That's bloody ridiculous.

Pause.

GUS. I bet he did it.

BEN. Who?

GUS. The brother.

BEN. I think you're right.

Pause.

(*Slamming down the paper.*) What about that, eh? A kid of eleven killing a cat and blaming it on his little sister of eight! It's enough to –

He breaks off in disgust and seizes the paper. GUS *rises.*

GUS. What time is he getting in touch?

BEN *reads.*

What time is he getting in touch?

BEN. What's the matter with you? It could be any time. Any time.

GUS (*moves to the foot of* BEN'S *bed*). Well, I was going to ask you something.

BEN. What?

GUS. Have you noticed the time that tank takes to fill?
BEN. What tank?
GUS. In the lavatory.
BEN. No. Does it?
GUS. Terrible.
BEN. Well, what about it?
GUS. What do you think's the matter with it?
BEN. Nothing.
GUS. Nothing?
BEN. It's got a deficient ballcock, that's all.
GUS. A deficient what?
BEN. Ballcock.
GUS. No? Really?
BEN. That's what I should say.
GUS. Go on! That didn't occur to me.

GUS *wanders to his bed and presses the mattress.*

I didn't have a very restful sleep today, did you? It's not much of a bed. I could have done with another blanket too. (*He catches sight of a picture on the wall.*) Hello, what's this? (*Peering at it.*) 'The First Eleven.' Cricketers. You seen this, Ben?

BEN (*reading*). What?
GUS. The first eleven.
BEN. What?
GUS. There's a photo here of the first eleven.
BEN. What first eleven?
GUS (*studying the photo*). It doesn't say.
BEN. What about that tea?
GUS. They all look a bit old to me.

GUS *wanders downstage, looks out front, then all about the room.*

I wouldn't like to live in this dump. I wouldn't mind if you had a window, you could see what it looked like outside.

BEN. What do you want a window for?

GUS. Well, I like to have a bit of a view, Ben. It whiles away the time.

He walks about the room.

I mean, you come into a place when it's still dark, you come into a room you've never seen before, you sleep all day, you do your job, and then you go away in the night again.

Pause.

I like to get a look at the scenery. You never get the chance in this job.

BEN. You get your holidays, don't you?

GUS. Only a fortnight.

BEN (*lowering the paper*). You kill me. Anyone would think you're working every day. How often do we do a job? Once a week? What are you complaining about?

GUS. Yes, but we've got to be on tap though, haven't we? You can't move out of the house in case a call comes.

BEN. You know what your trouble is?

GUS. What?

BEN. You haven't got any interests.

GUS. I've got interests.

BEN. What? Tell me one of your interests.

Pause.

GUS. I've got interests.

BEN. Look at me. What have I got?

GUS. I don't know. What?

BEN. I've got my woodwork. I've got my model boats. Have you ever seen me idle? I'm never idle. I know how to occupy my time, to its best advantage. Then when a call comes, I'm ready.

GUS. Don't you ever get a bit fed up?

BEN. Fed up? What with?

Silence.

BEN *reads.* GUS *feels in the pocket of his jacket, which hangs on the bed.*

GUS. You got any cigarettes? I've run out.

The lavatory flushes off left.

There she goes.

GUS *sits on his bed.*

No, I mean, I say the crockery's good. It is. It's very nice. But that's about all I can say for this place. It's worse than the last one. Remember that last place we were in? Last time, where was it? At least there was a wireless there. No, honest. He doesn't seem to bother much about our comfort these days.

BEN. When are you going to stop jabbering?

GUS. You'd get rheumatism in a place like this, if you stay long.

BEN. We're not staying long. Make the tea, will you? We'll be on the job in a minute.

GUS *picks up a small bag by his bed and brings out a packet of tea. He examines it and looks up.*

GUS. Eh, I've been meaning to ask you.

BEN. What the hell is it now?

GUS. Why did you stop the car this morning, in the middle of that road?

BEN (*lowering the paper*). I thought you were asleep.

GUS. I was, but I woke up when you stopped. You did stop, didn't you?

Pause.

In the middle of that road. It was still dark, don't you remember? I looked out. It was all misty. I thought perhaps you wanted to kip, but you were sitting up dead straight, like you were waiting for something.

BEN. I wasn't waiting for anything.

GUS. I must have fallen asleep again. What was all that about then? Why did you stop?

BEN (*picking up the paper*). We were too early.

GUS. Early? (*He rises.*) What do you mean? We got the call, didn't we, saying we were to start right away. We did. We shoved out on the dot. So how could we be too early?

BEN (*quietly*). Who took the call, me or you?

GUS. You.

BEN. We were too early.

GUS. Too early for what?

Pause.

You mean someone had to get out before we got in?

He examines the bedclothes.

I thought these sheets didn't look too bright. I thought they ponged a bit. I was too tired to notice when I got in this morning. Eh, that's taking a bit of a liberty, isn't it? I don't want to share my bed-sheets. I told you things were going down the drain. I mean, we've always had clean sheets laid on up till now. I've noticed it.

BEN. How do you know those sheets weren't clean?

GUS. What do you mean?

BEN. How do you know they weren't clean? You've spent the whole day in them, haven't you?

GUS. What, you mean it might be my pong? (*He sniffs sheets.*) Yes. (*He sits slowly on bed.*) It could be my pong, I suppose. It's difficult to tell. I don't really know what I pong like, that's the trouble.

BEN (*referring to the paper*). Kaw!

GUS. Eh, Ben.

BEN. Kaw!

GUS. Ben.

BEN. What?

GUS. What town are we in? I've forgotten.

BEN. I've told you. Birmingham.

GUS. Go on!

He looks with interest about the room.

That's in the Midlands. The second biggest city in Great Britain. I'd never have guessed.

He snaps his fingers.

Eh, it's Friday today, isn't it? It'll be Saturday tomorrow.

BEN. What about it?

GUS (*excited*). We could go and watch the Villa.

BEN. They're playing away.

GUS. No, are they? Caarr! What a pity.

BEN. Anyway, there's no time. We've got to get straight back.

GUS. Well, we have done in the past, haven't we? Stayed over and watched a game, haven't we? For a bit of relaxation.

BEN. Things have tightened up, mate. They've tightened up.

GUS *chuckles to himself.*

GUS. I saw the Villa get beat in a cup-tie once. Who was it against now? White shirts. It was one-all at half-time. I'll never forget it. Their opponents won by a penalty. Talk about drama. Yes, it was a disputed penalty. Disputed. They got beat two-one, anyway, because of it. You were there yourself.

BEN. Not me.

GUS. Yes, you were there. Don't you remember that disputed penalty?

BEN. No.

GUS. He went down just inside the area. Then they said he was just acting. I didn't think the other bloke touched him myself. But the referee had the ball on the spot.

BEN. Didn't touch him! What are you talking about? He laid him out flat!

GUS. Not the Villa. The Villa don't play that sort of game.

BEN. Get out of it.

Pause.

GUS. Eh, that must have been here, in Birmingham.

BEN. What must?

GUS. The Villa. That must have been here.

BEN. They were playing away.

GUS. Because you know who the other team was? It was the Spurs. It was Tottenham Hotspur.

BEN. Well, what about it?

GUS. We've never done a job in Tottenham.

BEN. How do you know?

GUS. I'd remember Tottenham.

BEN *turns on his bed to look at him.*

BEN. Don't make me laugh, will you?

BEN *turns back and reads.* GUS *yawns and speaks through his yawn.*

GUS. When's he going to get in touch?

Pause.

Yes, I'd like to see another football match. I've always been an ardent football fan. Here, what about coming to see the Spurs tomorrow?

BEN (*tonelessly*). They're playing away.

GUS. Who are?

BEN. The Spurs.

GUS. Then they might be playing here.

BEN. Don't be silly.

GUS. If they're playing away they might be playing here. They might be playing the Villa.

BEN (*tonelessly*). But the Villa are playing away.

Pause. An envelope slides under the door, right. GUS *sees it. He stands, looking at it.*

GUS. Ben.
BEN. Away. They're all playing away.
GUS. Ben, look here.
BEN. What?
GUS. Look.

BEN *turns his head and sees the envelope. He stands.*

BEN. What's that?
GUS. I don't know.
BEN. Where did it come from?
GUS. Under the door.
BEN. Well, what is it?
GUS. I don't know.

They stare at it.

BEN. Pick it up.
GUS. What do you mean?
BEN. Pick it up!

GUS *slowly moves towards it, bends and picks it up.*

What is it?
GUS. An envelope.
BEN. Is there anything on it?
GUS. No.
BEN. Is it sealed?
GUS. Yes.
BEN. Open it.
GUS. What?
BEN. Open it!

GUS *opens it and looks inside.*

What's in it?

GUS *empties twelve matches into his hand.*

GUS. Matches.

BEN. Matches?
GUS. Yes.
BEN. Show it to me.

GUS passes the envelope. BEN examines it.

Nothing on it. Not a word.
GUS. That's funny, isn't it?
BEN. It came under the door?
GUS. Must have done.
BEN. Well, go on.
GUS. Go on where?
BEN. Open the door and see if you can catch anyone outside.
GUS. Who, me?
BEN. Go on!

GUS stares at him, puts the matches in his pocket, goes to his bed and brings a revolver from under the pillow. He goes to the door, opens it, looks out and shuts it.

GUS. No one.

He replaces the revolver.

BEN. What did you see?
GUS. Nothing.
BEN. They must have been pretty quick.

GUS takes the matches from his pocket and looks at them.

GUS. Well, they'll come in handy.
BEN. Yes.
GUS. Won't they?
BEN. Yes, you're always running out, aren't you?
GUS. All the time.
BEN. Well, they'll come in handy then.
GUS. Yes.
BEN. Won't they?
GUS. Yes, I could do with them. I could do with them too.

BEN. You could, eh?

GUS. Yes.

BEN. Why?

GUS. We haven't got any.

BEN. Well, you've got some now, haven't you?

GUS. I can light the kettle now.

BEN. Yes, you're always cadging matches. How many have you got there?

GUS. About a dozen.

BEN. Well, don't lose them. Red too. You don't even need a box.

GUS *probes his ear with a match.*

(*Slapping his hand*). Don't waste them! Go on, go and light it.

GUS. Eh?

BEN. Go and light it.

GUS. Light what?

BEN. The kettle.

GUS. You mean the gas.

BEN. Who does?

GUS. You do.

BEN (*his eyes narrowing*). What do you mean, I mean the gas?

GUS. Well, that's what you mean, don't you? The gas.

BEN (*powerfully*). If I say go and light the kettle I mean go and light the kettle.

GUS. How can you light a kettle?

BEN. It's a figure of speech! Light the kettle. It's a figure of speech!

GUS. I've never heard it.

BEN. Light the kettle! It's common usage!

GUS. I think you've got it wrong.

BEN (*menacing*). What do you mean?

GUS. They say put on the kettle.

BEN (*taut*). Who says?

They stare at each other, breathing hard.

(*Deliberately.*) I have never in all my life heard anyone say put on the kettle.

GUS. I bet my mother used to say it.

BEN. Your mother? When did you last see your mother?

GUS. I don't know, about –

BEN. Well, what are you talking about your mother for?

They stare.

Gus, I'm not trying to be unreasonable. I'm just trying to point out something to you.

GUS. Yes, but –

BEN. Who's the senior partner here, me or you?

GUS. You.

BEN. I'm only looking after your interests, Gus. You've got to learn, mate.

GUS. Yes, but I've never heard –

BEN (*vehemently*). Nobody says light the gas! What does the gas light?

GUS. What does the gas –?

BEN (*grabbing him with two hands by the throat, at arm's length*). THE KETTLE, YOU FOOL!

GUS *takes the hands from his throat.*

GUS. All right, all right.

Pause.

BEN. Well, what are you waiting for?

GUS. I want to see if they light.

BEN. What?

GUS. The matches.

He takes out the flattened box and tries to strike.

No.

He throws the box under the bed.
BEN *stares at him.*

GUS *raises his foot.*

Shall I try it on here?

BEN *stares.* GUS *strikes a match on his shoe. It lights.*

Here we are.

BEN (*wearily*). Put on the bloody kettle, for Christ's sake.

BEN *goes to his bed, but, realising what he has said, stops and half turns. They look at each other.* GUS *slowly exits, left.* BEN *slams his paper down on the bed and sits on it, head in hands.*

GUS (*entering*). It's going.
BEN. What?
GUS. The stove.

GUS *goes to his bed and sits.*

I wonder who it'll be tonight.

Silence.

Eh, I've been wanting to ask you something.
BEN (*putting his legs on the bed*). Oh, for Christ's sake.
GUS. No. I was going to ask you something.

He rises and sits on BEN'S *bed.*

BEN. What are you sitting on my bed for?

GUS *sits.*

What's the matter with you? You're always asking me questions. What's the matter with you?
GUS. Nothing.
BEN. You never used to ask me so many damn questions. What's come over you?
GUS. No, I was just wondering.
BEN. Stop wondering. You've got a job to do . Why don't you just do it and shut up?

GUS. That's what I was wondering about.

BEN. What?

GUS. The job.

BEN. What job?

GUS (*tentatively*). I thought perhaps you might know something.

BEN *looks at him.*

I thought perhaps you – I mean – have you got any idea – who it's going to be tonight?

BEN. Who what's going to be?

They look at each other.

GUS (*at length*). Who it's going to be.

Silence.

BEN. Are you feeling all right?

GUS. Sure.

BEN. Go and make the tea.

GUS. Yes, sure.

GUS *exits, left,* BEN *looks after him. He then takes his revolver from under the pillow and checks it for ammunition.* GUS *re-enters.*

The gas has gone out.

BEN. Well, what about it?

GUS. There's a meter.

BEN. I haven't got any money.

GUS. Nor have I.

BEN. You'll have to wait.

GUS. What for?

BEN. For Wilson.

GUS. He might not come. He might just send a message. He doesn't always come.

BEN. Well, you'll have to do without it, won't you?

GUS. Blimey.

BEN. You'll have a cup of tea afterwards. What's the matter with you?

GUS. I like to have one before.

BEN *holds the revolver up to the light and polishes it.*

BEN. You'd better get ready anyway.

GUS. Well, I don't know, that's a bit much, you know, for my money.

He picks up a packet of tea from the bed and throws it into the bag.

I hope he's got a shilling, anyway, if he comes. He's entitled to have. After all, it's his place, he could have seen there was enough gas for a cup of tea.

BEN. What do you mean, it's his place?

GUS. Well, isn't it?

BEN. He's probably only rented it. It doesn't have to be his place.

GUS. I know it's his place. I bet the whole house is. He's not even laying on any gas now either.

GUS *sits on his bed.*

It's his place all right. Look at all the other places. You go to this address, there's a key there, there's a teapot, there's never a soul in sight – (*He pauses.*) Eh, nobody ever hears a thing, have you ever thought of that? We never get any complaints, do we, too much noise or anything like that? You never see a soul, do you? – except the bloke who comes. You ever noticed that? I wonder if the walls are sound-proof. (*He touches the wall above his bed.*) Can't tell. All you do is wait, eh? Half the time he doesn't even bother to put in an appearance, Wilson.

BEN. Why should he? He's a busy man.

GUS (*thoughtfully*). I find him hard to talk to, Wilson. Do you know that, Ben?

BEN. Scrub round it, will you?

Pause.

GUS. There are a number of things I want to ask him. But I can never get round to it, when I see him.

Pause.

I've been thinking about the last one.

BEN. What last one?

GUS. That girl.

BEN *grabs the paper, which he reads.*

(*Rising, looking down at* BEN). How many times have you read that paper?

BEN *slams the paper down and rises.*

BEN (*angrily*). What do you mean?

GUS. I was just wondering how many times you'd –

BEN. What are you doing, criticizing me?

GUS. No, I was just –

BEN. You'll get a swipe round your earhole if you don't watch your step.

GUS. Now look here, Ben –

BEN. I'm not looking anywhere! (*He addresses the room.*) How many times have I – ! A bloody liberty!

GUS. I didn't mean that.

BEN. You just get on with it, mate. Get on with it, that's all.

BEN *gets back on the bed.*

GUS. I was just thinking about that girl, that's all.

GUS *sits on his bed.*

She wasn't much to look at, I know, but still. It was a mess though, wasn't it? What a mess. Honest, I can't remember a mess like that one. They don't seem to hold together like men, women. A looser texture, like. Didn't she spread, eh? She didn't half spread. Kaw! But I've been meaning to ask you.

BEN *sits up and clenches his eyes.*

Who clears up after we've gone? I'm curious about that. Who does the clearing up? Maybe they don't clear up. Maybe they just leave them there, eh? What do you think? How many jobs have we done? Blimey, I can't count them. What if they never clear anything up after we've gone.

BEN (*pityingly*). You mutt. Do you think we're the only branch of this organization? Have a bit of common. They got departments for everything.

GUS. What cleaners and all?

BEN. You birk!

GUS. No, it was that girl made me start to think –

There is a loud clatter and racket in the bulge of wall between the beds, of something descending. They grab their revolvers, jump up and face the wall. The noise comes to a stop. Silence. They look at each other. BEN *gestures sharply towards the wall.* GUS *approaches the wall slowly. He bangs it with his revolver. It is hollow.* BEN *moves to the head of his bed, his revolver cocked.* GUS *puts his revolver on his bed and pats along the bottom of the centre panel. He finds a rim. He lifts the panel. Disclosed is a serving-hatch, a 'dumb waiter'. A wide box is held by pulleys.* GUS *peers into the box. He brings out a piece of paper.*

BEN. What is it?

GUS. You have a look at it.

BEN. Read it.

GUS (*reading*). Two braised steak and chips. Two sago puddings. Two teas without sugar.

BEN. Let me see that. (*He takes the paper.*)

GUS (*to himself*). Two teas without sugar.

BEN. Mmnn.
GUS. What do you think of that?
BEN. Well –

The box goes up. BEN *levels his revolver.*

GUS. Give us a chance! They're in a hurry, aren't they?

BEN *re-reads the note.* GUS *looks over his shoulder.*

That's a bit – that's a bit funny, isn't it?
BEN (*quickly*). No. It's not funny. It probably used to be a café here, that's all. Upstairs. These places change hands very quickly.
GUS. A café?
BEN. Yes.
GUS. What, you mean this was the kitchen, down here?
BEN. Yes, they change hands overnight, these places. Go into liquidation. The people who run it, you know, they don't find it a going concern, they move out.
GUS. You mean the people who ran this place didn't find it a going concern and moved out?
BEN. Sure.
GUS. WELL, WHO'S GOT IT NOW?

Silence.

BEN. What do you mean, who's got it now?
GUS. Who's got it now? If they moved out, who moved in?
BEN. Well, that all depends –

The box descends with a clatter and bang. BEN *levels his revolver.* GUS *goes to the box and brings out a piece of paper.*

GUS (*reading*). Soup of the day. Liver and onions. Jam tart.
A pause. GUS *looks at* BEN. BEN *takes the note and reads it. He walks slowly to the hatch.* GUS *follows.* BEN *looks into the hatch but not up it.* GUS *puts his hand on* BEN'S *shoulder.* BEN *throws it off.* GUS *puts his finger to his mouth. He leans*

on the hatch and swiftly looks up it. BEN *flings him away in alarm.* BEN *looks at the note. He throws his revolver on the bed and speaks with decision.*

BEN. We'd better send something up.
GUS. Eh?
BEN. We'd better send something up.
GUS. Oh! Yes. Yes. Maybe you're right.

They are both relieved at the decision.

BEN (*purposefully*). Quick! What have you got in that bag?
GUS. Not much.

GUS *goes to the hatch and shouts up it.*

Wait a minute!
BEN. Don't do that!

GUS *examines the contents of the bag and brings them out, one by one.*

GUS. Biscuits. A bar of chocolate. Half a pint of milk.
BEN. That all?
GUS. Packet of tea.
BEN. Good.
GUS. We can't send the tea. That's all the tea we've got.
BEN. Well, there's no gas. You can't do anything with it, can you?
GUS. Maybe they can send us down a bob.
BEN. What else is there?
GUS (*reaching into bag*). One Eccles cake.
BEN. One Eccles cake?
GUS. Yes.
BEN. You never told me you had an Eccles cake.
GUS. Didn't I?
BEN. Why only one? Didn't you bring one for me?
GUS. I didn't think you'd be keen.
BEN. Well, you can't send up one Eccles cake, anyway.

GUS. Why not?
BEN. Fetch one of those plates.
GUS. All right.

GUS goes towards the door, left, and stops.

Do you mean I can keep the Eccles cake then?
BEN. Keep it?
GUS. Well, they don't know we've got it, do they?
BEN. That's not the point.
GUS. Can't I keep it?
BEN. No, you can't. Get the plate.

GUS exits, left. BEN looks in the bag. He brings out a packet of crisps. Enter GUS with a plate.

(*Accusingly, holding up the crisps*). Where did these come from?
GUS. What?
BEN. Where did these crisps come from?
GUS. Where did you find them?
BEN (*hitting him on the shoulder*). You're playing a dirty game, my lad!
GUS. I only eat those with beer!
BEN. Well, where were you going to get the beer?
GUS. I was saving them till I did.
BEN. I'll remember this. Put everything on the plate.

They pile everything on to the plate. The box goes up without the plate.

Wait a minute!

They stand.

GUS. It's gone up.
BEN. It's all your stupid fault, playing about!
GUS. What do we do now?
BEN. We'll have to wait till it comes down.

BEN *puts the plate on the bed, puts on his shoulder holster, and starts to put on his tie.*

You'd better get ready.

GUS *goes to his bed, puts on his tie, and starts to fix his holster.*

GUS. Hey, Ben.
BEN. What?
GUS. What's going on here?

Pause.

BEN. What do you mean?
GUS. How can this be a café?
BEN. It used to be a café.
GUS. Have you seen the gas stove?
BEN. What about it?
GUS. It's only got three rings.
BEN. So what?
GUS. Well, you couldn't cook much on three rings, not for a busy place like this.
BEN (*irritably*). That's why the service is slow!

BEN *puts on his waistcoat.*

GUS. Yes, but what happens when we're not here? What do they do then? All these menus coming down and nothing going up. It might have been going on like this for years.

BEN *brushes his jacket.*

What happens when we go?

BEN *puts on his jacket.*

They can't do much business.

The box descends. They turn about. GUS *goes to the hatch and brings out a note.*

GUS (*reading*). Macaroni Pastitsio. Ormitha Macarounada.
BEN. What was that?
GUS. Macaroni Pastitsio. Ormitha Macarounada.
BEN. Greek dishes.
GUS. No.
BEN. That's right.
GUS. That's pretty high class.
BEN. Quick before it goes up.

GUS *puts the plate in the box.*

GUS (*calling up the hatch*). Three McVitie and Price! One Lyons Red Label! One Smith's Crisps! One Eccles cake! One Fruit and Nut!
BEN. Cadbury's.
GUS (*up the hatch*). Cadbury's!
BEN (*handing the milk*). One bottle of milk.
GUS (*up the hatch*). One bottle of milk! Half a pint! (*He looks at the label.*) Express Dairy! (*He puts the bottle in the box.*)

The box goes up.

Just did it.
BEN. You shouldn't shout like that.
GUS. Why not?
BEN. It isn't done.

BEN *goes to his bed.*

Well, that should be all right, anyway, for the time being.
GUS. You think so, eh?
BEN. Get dressed, will you? It'll be any minute now.

GUS *puts on his waistcoat.* BEN *lies down and looks up at the ceiling.*

GUS. This is some place. No tea and no biscuits.
BEN. Eating makes you lazy, mate. You're getting lazy, you know that? You don't want to get slack on your job.

GUS. Who me?

BEN. Slack, mate, slack.

GUS. Who me? Slack?

BEN. Have you checked your gun? You haven't even checked your gun. It looks disgraceful, anyway. Why don't you ever polish it?

GUS *rubs his revolver on the sheet.* BEN *takes out a pocket mirror and straightens his tie.*

GUS. I wonder where the cook is. They must have had a few, to cope with that. Maybe they had a few more gas stoves. Eh! Maybe there's another kitchen along the passage.

BEN. Of course there is! Do you know what it takes to make an Ormitha Macarounada?

GUS. No, what?

BEN. An Ormitha –! Buck your ideas up, will you?

GUS. Takes a few cooks, eh?

GUS *puts his revolver in its holster.*

The sooner we're out of this place the better.

He puts on his jacket.

Why doesn't he get in touch? I feel like I've been here years. (*He takes his revolver out of its holster to check the ammunition.*) We've never let him down though, have we? We've never let him down. I was thinking only the other day, Ben. We're reliable, aren't we?

He puts his revolver back in its holster.

Still, I'll be glad when it's over tonight.

He brushes his jacket.

I hope the bloke's not going to get excited tonight, or anything. I'm feeling a bit off. I've got a splitting headache.

Silence.

The box descends. BEN *jumps up.*

GUS *collects the note.*

(*Reading.*) One Bamboo Shoots, Water Chestnuts and Chicken. One Char Siu and Beansprouts.

BEN. Beansprouts?

GUS. Yes.

BEN. Blimey.

GUS. I wouldn't know where to begin.

He looks back at the box. The packet of tea is inside it. He picks it up.

They've sent back the tea.

BEN (*anxious*). What'd they do that for?

GUS. Maybe it isn't tea-time.

The box goes up. Silence.

BEN (*throwing the tea on the bed, and speaking urgently*). Look here. We'd better tell them.

GUS. Tell them what?

BEN. That we can't do it, we haven't got it.

GUS. All right then.

BEN. Lend us your pencil. We'll write a note.

GUS, *turning for a pencil, suddenly discovers the speaking-tube, which hangs on the right wall of the hatch facing his bed.*

GUS. What's this?

BEN. What?

GUS. This.

BEN (*examining it*). This? It's a speaking-tube.

GUS. How long has that been there?

BEN. Just the job. We should have used it before, instead of shouting up there.

GUS. Funny I never noticed it before.

BEN. Well, come on.

GUS. What do you do?

BEN. See that? That's a whistle.
GUS. What, this?
BEN. Yes, take it out. Pull it out.

GUS *does so.*

That's it.
GUS. What do we do now?
BEN. Blow into it.
GUS. Blow?
BEN. It whistles up there if you blow. Then they know you want to speak. Blow.

GUS *blows. Silence.*

GUS (*tube at mouth*). I can't hear a thing.
BEN. Now you speak! Speak into it!

GUS *looks at* BEN, *then speaks into the tube.*

GUS. The larder's bare!
BEN. Give me that!

He grabs the tube and puts it to his mouth.

(*Speaking with great deference.*) Good evening. I'm sorry to – bother you, but we just thought we'd better let you know that we haven't got anything left. We sent up all we had. There's no more food down here.

He brings the tube slowly to his ear.

What?

To mouth.

What?

To ear. He listens. To mouth.

No, all we had we sent up.

To ear. He listens. To mouth.

Oh, I'm very sorry to hear that.

To ear. He listens. To GUS.

The Eccles cake was stale.

He listens. To GUS.

The chocolate was melted.

He listens. To GUS.

The milk was sour.
GUS. What about the crisps?
BEN (*listening*). The biscuits were mouldy.

He glares at GUS. *Tube to mouth.*

Well, we're very sorry about that.

Tube to ear.

What?

To mouth.

What?

To ear.

Yes. Yes.

To mouth.

Yes certainly. Certainly. Right away.

To ear. The voice has ceased. He hangs up the tube.

(*Excitedly*). Did you hear that?

GUS. What?
BEN. You know what he said? Light the kettle! Not put on the kettle! Not light the gas! But light the kettle!
GUS. How can we light the kettle?
BEN. What do you mean?

GUS. There's no gas.
BEN (*clapping hand to head*). Now what do we do?
GUS. What did he want us to light the kettle for?
BEN. For tea. He wanted a cup of tea.
GUS. *He* wanted a cup of tea! What about me? I've been wanting a cup of tea all night!
BEN (*despairingly*). What do we do now?
GUS. What are we supposed to drink?

BEN *sits on his bed, staring.*

What about us?

BEN *sits.*

I'm thirsty too. I'm starving. And he wants a cup of tea. That beats the band, that does.

BEN *lets his head sink on to his chest.*

I could do with a bit of sustenance myself. What about you? You look as if you could do with something too.

GUS *sits on his bed.*

We send him up all we've got and he's not satisfied. No, honest, it's enough to make the cat laugh. Why did you send him up all that stuff? (*Thoughtfully.*) Why did I send it up?

Pause.

Who knows what he's got upstairs? He's probably got a salad bowl. They must have something up there. They won't get much from down here. You notice they didn't ask for any salads? They've probably got a salad bowl up there. Cold meat, radishes, cucumbers. Watercress. Roll mops.

Pause.

Hardboiled eggs.

Pause.

The lot. They've probably got a crate of beer too. Probably eating my crisps with a pint of beer now. Didn't have anything to say about those crisps, did he? They do all right, don't worry about that. You don't think they're just going to sit there and wait for stuff to come up from down here, do you? That'll get them nowhere.

Pause.

They do all right.

Pause.

And he wants a cup of tea.

Pause.

That's past a joke, in my opinion.

He looks over at BEN, *rises, and goes to him.*

What's the matter with you? You don't look too bright. I feel like an Alka-Seltzer myself.

BEN *sits up.*

BEN (*in a low voice*). Time's getting on.

GUS. I know. I don't like doing a job on an empty stomach.

BEN (*wearily*). Be quiet a minute. Let me give you your instructions.

GUS. What for? We always do it the same way, don't we?

BEN. Let me give you your instructions.

GUS *sighs and sits next to* BEN *on the bed. The instructions are stated and repeated automatically.*

When we get the call, you go over and stand behind the door.

GUS. Stand behind the door.

BEN. If there's a knock on the door you don't answer it.

GUS. If there's a knock on the door I don't answer it.

BEN. But there won't be a knock on the door.

GUS. So I won't answer it.
BEN. When the bloke comes in –
GUS. When the bloke comes in –
BEN. Shut the door behind him.
GUS. Shut the door behind him.
BEN. Without divulging your presence.
GUS. Without divulging my presence.
BEN. He'll see me and come towards me.
GUS. He'll see you and come towards you.
BEN. He won't see you.
GUS (*absently*). Eh?
BEN. He won't see you.
GUS. He won't see me.
BEN. But he'll see me.
GUS. He'll see you.
BEN. He won't know you're there.
GUS. He won't know you're there.
BEN. He won't know *you're* there.
GUS. He won't know I'm there.
BEN. I take out my gun.
GUS. You take out your gun.
BEN. He stops in his tracks.
GUS. He stops in his tracks.
BEN. If he turns round –
GUS. If he turns round –
BEN. You're there.
GUS. I'm here.

BEN *frowns and presses his forehead.*

You've missed something out.
BEN. I know. What?
GUS. I haven't taken my gun out, according to you.
BEN. You take your gun out –
GUS. After I've closed the door.
BEN. After you've closed the door.

GUS. You've never missed that out before, you know that?
BEN. When he sees you behind him –
GUS. Me behind him –
BEN. And me in front of him –
GUS. And you in front of him –
BEN. He'll feel uncertain –
GUS. Uneasy.
BEN. He won't know what to do.
GUS. So what will he do?
BEN. He'll look at me and he'll look at you.
GUS. We won't say a word.
BEN. We'll look at him.
GUS. He won't say a word.
BEN. He'll look at us.
GUS. And we'll look at him.
BEN. Nobody says a word.

Pause.

GUS. What do we do if it's a girl?
BEN. We do the same.
GUS. Exactly the same?
BEN. Exactly.

Pause.

GUS. We don't do anything different?
BEN. We do exactly the same.
GUS. Oh.

GUS *rises, and shivers.*

Excuse me.

He exits through the door on the left. BEN *remains sitting on the bed, still.*
The lavatory chain is pulled once off left, but the lavatory does not flush.
Silence.

GUS *re-enters and stops inside the door, deep in thought. He looks at* BEN, *then walks slowly across to his own bed. He is troubled. He stands, thinking. He turns and looks at* BEN. *He moves a few paces towards him.*

(*Slowly in a low, tense voice.*) Why did he send us matches if he knew there was no gas?

Silence.

BEN *stares in front of him.* GUS *crosses to the left side of* BEN, *to the foot of his bed, to get to his other ear.*

Ben. Why did he send us matches if he knew there was no gas?

BEN *looks up.*

Why did he do that?

BEN. Who?

GUS. Who sent us those matches?

BEN. What are you talking about?

GUS *stares down at him.*

GUS (*thickly*). Who is it upstairs?

BEN (*nervously*). What's one thing to do with another?

GUS. Who is it, though?

BEN. What's one thing to do with another?

BEN *fumbles for his paper on the bed.*

GUS. I asked you a question.

BEN. Enough!

GUS (*with growing agitation*). I asked you before. Who moved in? I asked you. You said the people who had it before moved out. Well, who moved in?

BEN (*hunched*). Shut up.

GUS. I told you, didn't I?

BEN (*standing*). Shut up!

GUS (*feverishly*). I told you before who owned this place, didn't I? I told you.

BEN *hits him viciously on the shoulder.*

I told you who ran this place, didn't I?

BEN *hits him viciously on the shoulder.*

(*Violently.*) Well, what's he playing all these games for? That's what I want to know. What's he doing it for?

BEN. What games?

GUS (*passionately, advancing*). What's he doing it for? We've been through our tests, haven't we? We got right through our tests, years ago, didn't we? We took them together, don't you remember, didn't we? We've proved ourselves before now, haven't we? We've always done our job. What's he doing all this for? What's the idea? What's he playing these games for?

The box in the shaft comes down behind them. The noise is this time accompanied by a shrill whistle, as it falls. GUS *rushes to the hatch and seizes the note.*

(*Reading.*) Scampi!

He crumples the note, picks up the tube, takes out the whistle, blows and speaks.

WE'VE GOT NOTHING LEFT! NOTHING! DO YOU UNDERSTAND?

BEN *seizes the tube and flings* GUS *away. He follows* GUS *and slaps him hard, back-handed, across the chest.*

BEN. Stop it! You maniac!

GUS. But you heard!

BEN (*savagely*). That's enough! I'm warning you!

Silence.

BEN *hangs the tube. He goes to his bed and lies down. He picks up his paper and reads.*

Silence.
The box goes up.
They turn quickly, their eyes meet. BEN *turns to his paper.*
Slowly GUS *goes back to his bed, and sits.*
Silence.
The hatch falls back into place.
They turn quickly, their eyes meet. BEN *turns back to his paper.*
Silence.
BEN *throws his paper down.*

BEN. Kaw!

He picks up the paper and looks at it.

Listen to this!

Pause.

What about that, eh?

Pause.

Kaw!

Pause.

Have you ever heard such a thing?
GUS (*dully*). Go on!
BEN. It's true.
GUS. Get away.
BEN. It's down here in black and white.
GUS (*very low*). Is that a fact?
BEN. Can you imagine it.
GUS. It's unbelievable.
BEN. It's enough to make you want to puke, isn't it?
GUS (*almost inaudible*). Incredible.

BEN *shakes his head. He puts the paper down and rises. He fixes the revolver in his holster.*

GUS *stands up. He goes towards the door on the left.*

BEN. Where are you going?
GUS. I'm going to have a glass of water.

He exits. BEN *brushes dust off his clothes and shoes. The whistle in the speaking-tube blows. He goes to it, takes the whistle out and puts the tube to his ear. He listens. He puts it to his mouth.*

BEN. Yes.

To ear. He listens. To mouth.

Straight away. Right.

To ear. He listens. To mouth.

Sure we're ready.

To ear. He listens. To mouth.

Understood. Repeat. He has arrived and will be coming in straight away. The normal method to be employed. Understood.

To ear. He listens. To mouth.

Sure we're ready.

To ear. He listens. To mouth.

Right.

He hangs the tube up.

Gus!

He takes out a comb and combs his hair, adjusts his jacket to diminish the bulge of the revolver. The lavatory flushes off left. BEN *goes quickly to the door, left.*

Gus!